EASY PIANO

Classical Themes
FOR KIDS

On the Cover:
The Daughters of Catulle Mendès (1888)
by Pierre-Auguste Renoir (1841–1919)

ISBN 978-1-5400-9490-2

Visit Hal Leonard Online at
www.halleonard.com

Contact us:
Hal Leonard
7777 West Bluemound Road
Milwaukee, WI 53213
Email: info@halleonard.com

In Europe, contact:
Hal Leonard Europe Limited
42 Wigmore Street
Marylebone, London, W1U 2RN
Email: info@halleonardeurope.com

In Australia, contact:
Hal Leonard Australia Pty. Ltd.
4 Lentara Court
Cheltenham, Victoria, 3192 Australia
Email: info@halleonard.com.au

Contents

Song Notes

Air on the G String
BY J.S. BACH

"Air" became known as "Air on the G String" when the violinist and teacher August Wilhelmj arranged the melody by transposing it to C Major and lowering it an octave, which allowed the tune to be played entirely on only one string. In this keyboard arrangement the right-hand melody is written using ledger lines between the treble and bass staves. Remember that the ledger line closest to the staff is Middle C, and read the notes by interval from this landmark. Play left hand steadily and with a full, round tone. Think of imitating the sound of cellos and basses in the orchestra.

By the Beautiful Blue Danube
BY JOHANN STRAUSS, JR.

Strauss was known as the waltz "king" and this selection is his most popular composition. A waltz is a dance in triple meter, with the accent on the first beat of the measure. The dancers take a step on each beat of the music, turning in a circular pattern. Practice the left hand with a slight emphasis on the first quarter-note beat. The half notes on beat 2 should be played with less emphasis than the quarter note. The right hand should be strongly singing throughout and played in a spirited manner.

Canon in D
BY JOHANN PACHELBEL

Although the exact date is unknown, "Canon in D" was written between 1680 and 1706, becoming one of the most popular pieces in classical music, so popular that it influenced and was sampled by pop artists like Aphrodite's Child, Pet Shop Boys, Green Day, Transiberian Orchestra and Maroon 5. As you study this arrangement, you'll notice a repeating chord pattern, outlined in the bass: D-A-Bm-F♯m-G-D-G-A. Add the right hand in eight-measure sections paying special attention to changes in texture and rhythm.

CLAIR DE LUNE
BY CLAUDE DEBUSSY

"Clair de Lune" translates to "Moonlight" and is said to be inspired by a poem by Paul Verlaie. This well-known tune has been orchestrated and arranged for various instruments by a wide variety of musicians. You'll notice the direction "With pedal" at the beginning of the piece. Written during the Impressionist period, Debussy wanted to create, with music, a wash of color like Impressionist painters of the time. Listen to the wash of sound you create while holding down the pedal, lifting fully, or partially, as the left-hand chords change.

Dance of the Sugar Plum Fairy
BY PYOTR IL'YICH TCHAIKOVSKY

"Dance of the Sugar Plum Fairy" is from the famous ballet *The Nutcracker*. In the orchestra this theme is played on the celeste. The celeste is a small keyboard instrument with a distinctive bell-like sound, described by many as a combination of a toy piano and a glockenspiel. Listen to a recording of a celeste if you can, to hear this unique instrument. Play with a light and delicate touch, and with a sense of forward motion.

Ein Mädchen oder Weibchen
BY WOLFGANG AMADEUS MOZART

Papageno's aria from the opera *The Magic Flute* is a lilting melody full of playful motives. He sings of his desire for love and companionship. Practice the right-hand melody until you can play it easily, noting the dotted eighth-note rhythms and the short sixteenth-note figures. The tempo slows, and the time signature changes to 6/8 in measure 13. Don't hesitate to add a little drama with the *rit.* (slowing the tempo) and fermata in measures 22–23, and with the *rit.* in the last two measures.

Eine kleine Nachtmusik
BY WOLFGANG AMADEUS MOZART

This arrangement is an excerpt, or portion, of a larger work, *Serenade No. 13 for Strings*. *Allegro* means quickly, but practice at a slow tempo first. After the *forte* opening chord, hands play in unison until measure 4, when the left hand supports the melody with repeated chords. As you move from chord to chord, notice which notes stay the same. The dynamic changes add color and excitement.

The Flight of the Bumblebee
BY NIKOLAI RIMSKY-KORSAKOV

Written as an orchestral interlude, "Flight of the Bumblebee" sounds like the seemingly random and anxious flying of this beautiful but sometimes annoying insect. This tune is one of classical music's most familiar works and is often referenced and used in pop culture. The right hand might look difficult, but with careful attention you'll be able to play this up to tempo in no time. Divide the measures of running sixteenth notes into eight-measure sections. The B section, beginning in measure 17 provides a contrast until A returns at measure 41 to keep you "buzzing" until the end.

Hornpipe
BY GEORGE FRIDERIC HANDEL

"Hornpipe" is a selection from Handel's orchestral suite *Water Music*. Historians say the suite was written for an outdoor performance requested by King George I in 1717. A hornpipe is a folk dance in triple meter. Although the texture is thin (each hand only playing single lines most of the time) both treble and bass lines are independent of each other. For this reason, most of your practice should be hands alone until you are comfortable with each line.

Largo from Symphony No. 9
BY ANTONÍN DVOŘÁK

"Largo" is one of the themes from Dvořák's *Symphony No. 9*, "From the New World," also known as the *New World Symphony*. Dvořák was living in the United States when he wrote the symphony and was inspired by the music and culture he experienced there. *Largo* is translated as a very slow tempo, to be played in a dignified manner. After the four-measure introduction, the theme begins with its distinctive dotted rhythm. Keep a steady quarter note beat throughout each measure, playing the eighth note gently, not accented.

Liebestraum No. 3
BY FRANZ LISZT

"Liebestraum" (Dream of Love) is from a set of three solo piano pieces. The third of the set is the most well-known. Play the beautiful, soaring melody in the right hand with a full, rounded tone. The left hand accompanies the melody with single notes in a broken-chord style. The right hand often makes use of a lower voice; listen carefully to balance the melody. In measures 57 and 65 the squiggled line that extends from bass to treble clef indicates an *arpeggiated* effect. Play each note one at a time from bottom to top, as if strummed on a string instrument.

Morning
BY EDVARD GRIEG

This melody was written for a play by Henrik Ibsen titled *Peer Gynt* and is included in Grieg's *Peer Gynt Suite* for orchestra. Peer Gynt is a character in Norwegian folktales, and the play tells of his journeys from the Norwegian mountains to the African desert. This beautiful, calm melody is accompanied by left-hand triads. Really sink into the triads, listening for all three notes to sound at the same time. From measure 41 to the end, the accompaniment changes to "broken" chords, meaning that instead of playing all three notes of the chord at the same time, the notes are played one at a time.

Pavane for the Sleeping Beauty
BY MAURICE RAVEL

A pavane is a slow, stylized dance from the Renaissance period. "Pavane for the Sleeping Beauty" is the first movement of Ravel's *Mother Goose Suite* for piano duet. This arrangement is not a duet, but an arrangement of the Sleeping Beauty theme. Imagine the dancers' steps as you play the melody. Plan how softly you will play at the *pianissimo* sections. Can you make a contrast between *piano* and *pianissimo*?

Pomp and Circumstance
BY EDWARD ELGAR

The definition of "Pomp and Circumstance" is: Impressive formal activities or ceremonies. Our arrangement by Edward Elgar is one of a series called *Pomp and Circumstance Military Marches*, though over time this march has been played more for graduations than the military. Set a solemn tone and a steady beat. Left hand plays various intervals. As you sight read them, notice which notes change from measure to measure; often at least one note stays the same. Allow the steady quarter notes to keep the beat.

PROMENADE THEME
BY MODEST MOUSSORGSKY

"Promenade Theme" is from the famous piano solo *Pictures at an Exhibition*, depicting a journey through an art museum with movements such as "The Gnome," "The Old Castle," "Catacombs," "The Great Gate of Kiev" and others. "Promenade" appears five times throughout the piece. Notice how often the meter changes, sometimes from measure to measure, until settling with 6/4 in measure 12. Allow this to help you imagine walking through the museum, using the quarter-note beat to keep the tempo steady.

RHAPSODY IN BLUE
BY GEORGE GERSHWIN

"Rhapsody in Blue" was written in 1924 and is recognized as one of the most popular pieces in American music. Gershwin's biographer, Isaac Goldberg, wrote that Gershwin said about the piece, "I heard it as a sort of musical kaleidoscope of America." A rhapsody is a single movement work in irregular form, with improvisatory passages and many contrasts, along with the use of *rubato*, a push and pull of the tempo. Before you begin working on this arrangement, listen to a recording of the original piece to get a feel for the character of each of the different sections. Work carefully section by section before putting the whole piece together.

Ride of the Valkyries
BY RICHARD WAGNER

Wagner's "Ride of the Valkyries" is the prelude to Act 3 of his opera *Die Walküre*. In Norse mythology a Valkyrie is a female figure charged with bringing the chosen to Valhalla, the afterlife hall of the slain. The Valkerie's battle cry is portrayed with the dotted eighth-sixteenth-eighth figure on the third quarter-note beat in each measure. (You can count this arrangement in 3, with each dotted quarter note getting the beat.) This figure propels the melody rhythmically, and melodically climbs higher each time it's presented, creating excitement and tension. Play this arrangement with energy and strength, in the spirit of the Valkerie!

SLEEPING BEAUTY WALTZ
BY PYOTR IL'YICH TCHAIKOVSKY

Part of Tchaikovsky's ballet suite, *The Sleeping Beauty*, this stunning waltz is loved the world over. In the ballet, the waltz is performed at Princess Aurora's 16th birthday celebration, and in the Disney movie of the same name, the song "Once Upon a Dream" is based on this melody. Enjoy the left-hand waltz-bass pattern, practicing this part alone until you are very familiar with the moving bass notes. Next add the majestic right-hand melody, playing with a full, singing tone. Beginning in measure 32, take extra care reading the accidentals (sharps and flats) and use the fingering provided.

SPRING
BY ANTONIO VIVALDI

"Spring" is one of a group of four violin concerti published in 1725, each representing a season of the year. This work is unique in that Vivaldi paid special care to relate his music to the sights and sounds of each season in addition to linking them to poetry, quite possibly written by himself. Here's a stanza of poetry linked to "Spring."

Spring has arrived with you,
welcomed by the birds with happy songs,
and the brooks, amidst gentle breezes,
murmur sweetly as they flow.

Keep a loose, bouncy wrist when playing the sixteenth-note figures in the right hand. Set a steady tempo, not too fast, so that you can keep the sixteenths perfectly in time. Scan through the left-hand part before you play it. You'll see an abundance of the bass clef note E, making this part as easy as a spring breeze!

STARS AND STRIPES FOREVER
BY JOHN PHILIP SOUSA

Considered to be his greatest work, "Stars and Stripes Forever" is a patriotic march first performed on May 14, 1897, becoming the official National March of the United States by an act of the U.S. Congress. In standard military march form, melodies repeat in sections called strains, a hallmark of Sousa's style. The slanted lines between the clefs show that the melody moves from treble to bass and back again.

The Swan
BY CAMILLE SAINT-SAËNS

"The Swan," from *The Carnival of the Animals*, is best known as a cello solo. Historians say that it's the only movement of this work that Saint-Saëns allowed played in public during his lifetime, believing the other movements were too frivolous to be associated with a serious composer. This beautiful, singing melody is written in the treble clef in our arrangement; listening to a recording of solo cello will give you great insight into how to shape the phrases to create long, flowing lines.

Symphony No. 5
BY LUDWIG VAN BEETHOVEN

Beethoven's fifth symphony is one of the most popular symphonies of all time. In this collection we've included themes from the first movement. The opening theme, with the famously distinctive "short-short-short-long" was said (by Beethoven himself) to be "fate knocking at the door." Hands play together in unison for the first four measures. There are an abundance of repeated notes and intervals that leap and fall. Read through the music at a slow tempo, looking for patterns. The final measures bring back the dramatic first theme, so finish with a flourish!

TOREADOR SONG
BY GEORGES BIZET

"Toreador Song," from the opera *Carmen*, is sung by the bullfighter, describing his experiences in the ring, the cheering crowds, and the thrill of victory. Play the dotted eighth-sixteenth rhythm with a jaunty confidence, as if you were wearing the bullfighter's cape. Keep the left-hand quarter-note rhythm steady, as a solid backdrop to the unfolding drama.

Träumerei
BY ROBERT SCHUMANN

"Träumerei" (Dreaming) is from *Kinderszenen* (Scenes from Childhood), written in 1838. Schumann, a composer during the Romantic period, is well known for his delicate, masterful piano miniatures. Listen to the dreamy, lyrical melody in the right hand. Practice with extreme legato, making use of the fingering given. The left-hand lines are just as lyrical, so practice the left-hand part in the same way. The performance tempo of this piece is, "Slowly, with expression," calling for great control and sensitivity. Practice small sections in a VERY slow tempo until you have mastered them.

William Tell Overture
BY GIOACHINO ROSSINI

This overture to the opera *William Tell* has been widely heard in both classical and popular musical culture, most famously as the theme music for *The Lone Ranger* radio and television shows. This exciting melody is instantly recognizable, and requires crisp, clean technique in the right hand. Practice slowly, with a light, almost staccato touch, working in eight-measure sections. Use a metronome to help increase the tempo. You have a bit of a break from the constant motion beginning in measure 17, so sink into the chords but don't let the tempo slow down. Allow for a dramatic pause at measure 26 before galloping to the end of the piece with extra energy and drive.

Air on the G String

FROM ORCHESTRAL SUITE NO. 3 IN D MAJOR

By JOHANN SEBASTIAN BACH
(1685–1750)

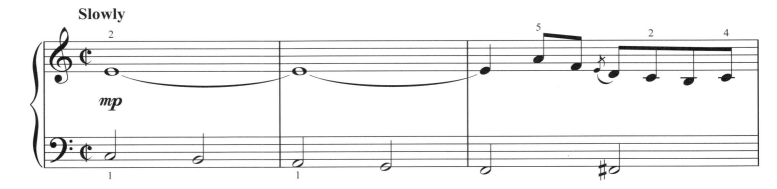

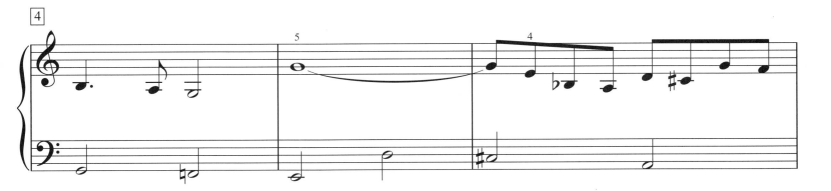

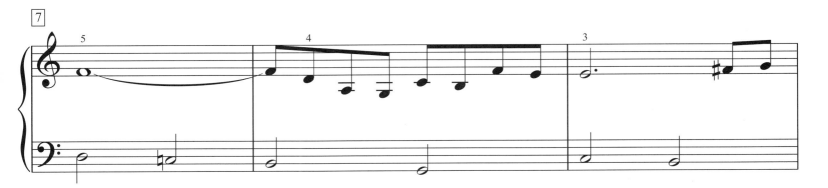

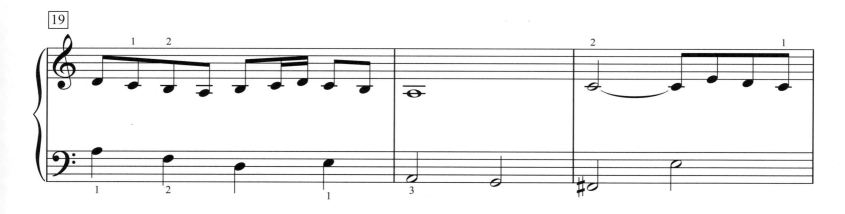

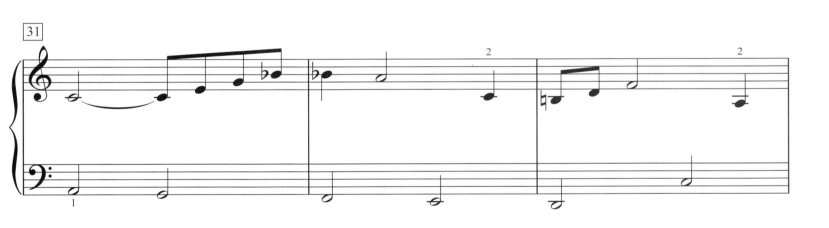

By the Beautiful Blue Danube

By JOHANN STRAUSS, JR.
(1825–1899)

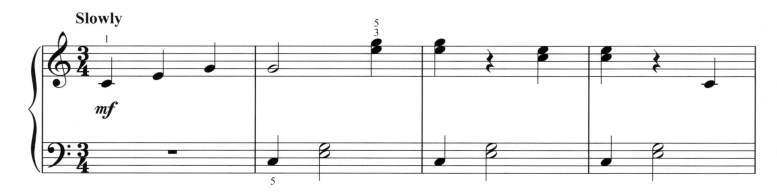

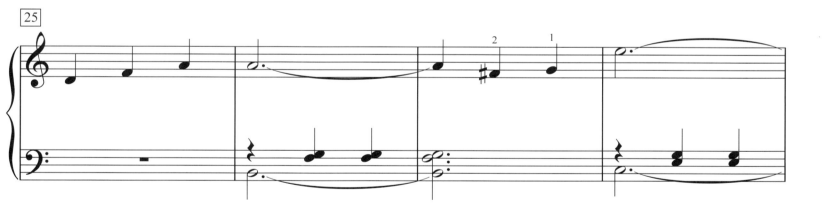

Fine

D.C. al Fine

Canon in D

By JOHANN PACHELBEL
(1653–1706)

Clair de Lune

By CLAUDE DEBUSSY
(1862–1918)

Moderately

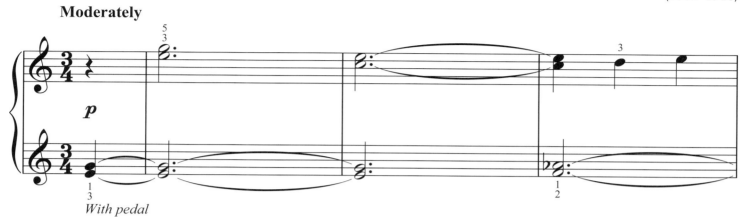

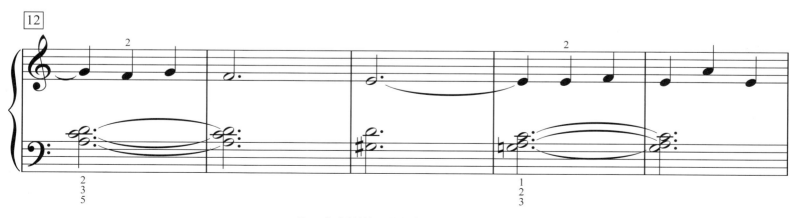

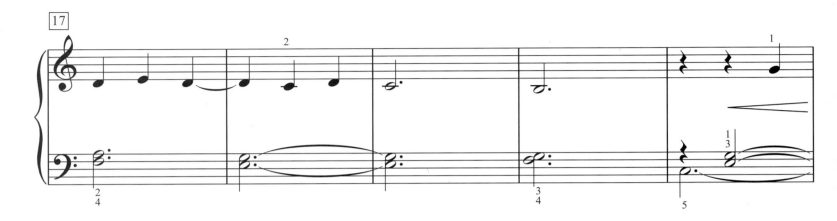

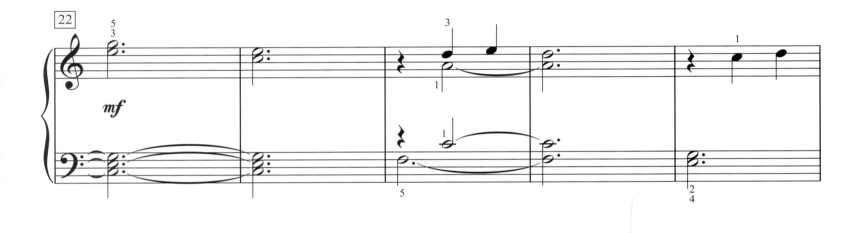

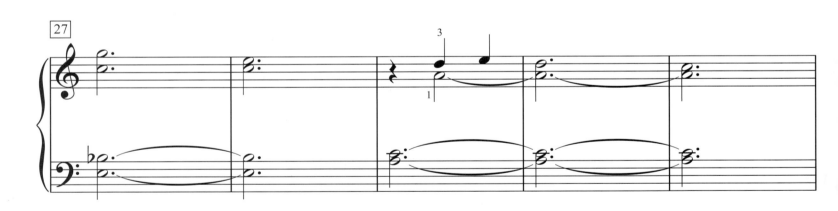

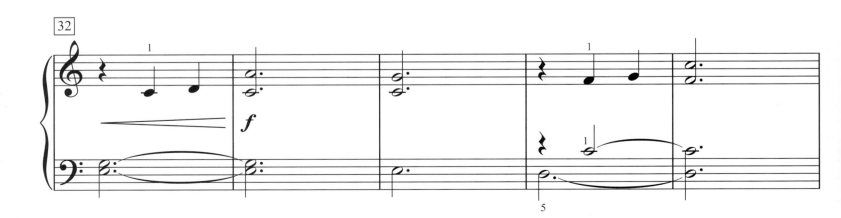

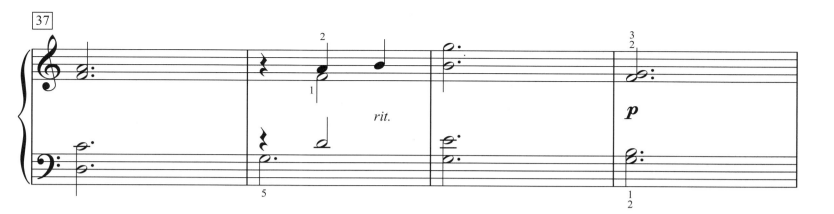

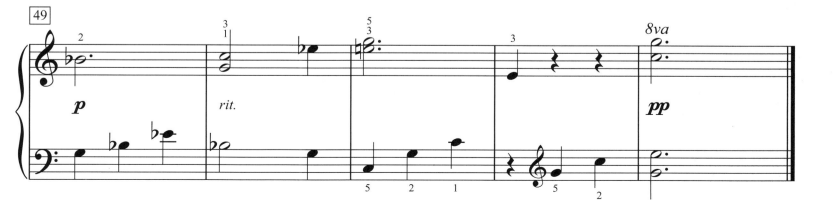

Dance of the Sugar Plum Fairy

FROM THE NUTCRACKER SUITE

By PYOTR IL'YICH TCHAIKOVSKY
(1840–1893)

Daintily, not too slow

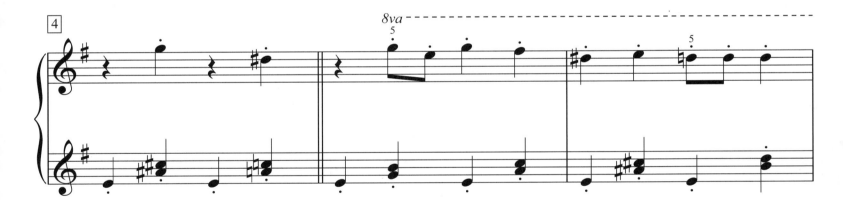

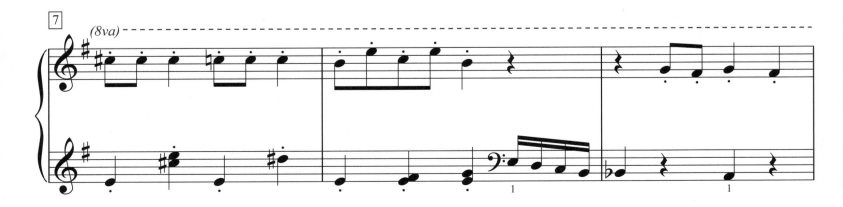

Ein Mädchen oder Weibchen

Papageno's Aria from THE MAGIC FLUTE

By WOLFGANG AMADEUS MOZART
(1756–1791)

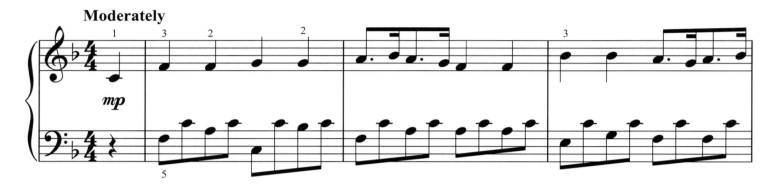

Eine kleine Nachtmusik
(A Little Night Music)
First Movement Excerpt

By WOLFGANG AMADEUS MOZART
(1756–1791)

Allegro

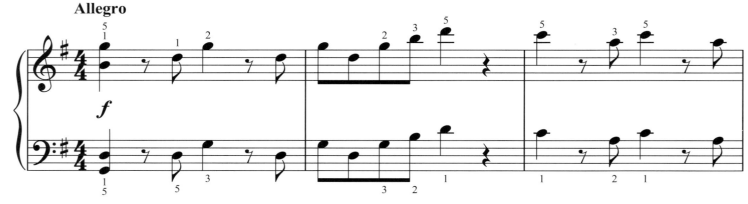

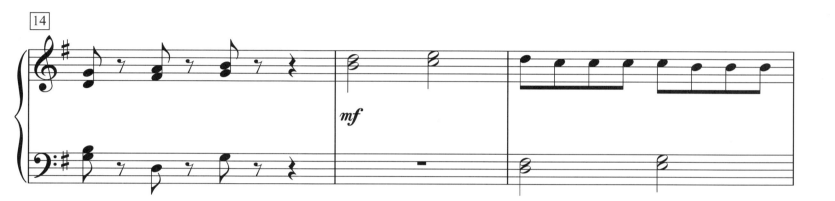

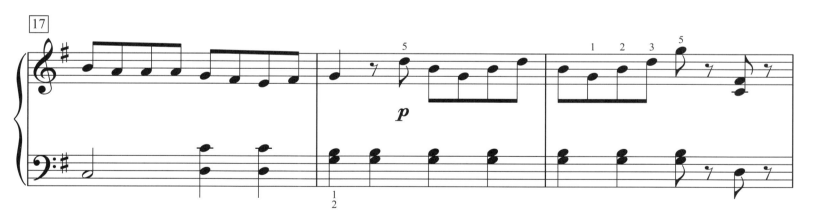

The Flight of the Bumblebee

By NIKOLAI RIMSKY-KORSAKOV
(1844–1908)

Hornpipe

FROM WATER MUSIC

By GEORGE FRIDERIC HANDEL
(1685–1759)

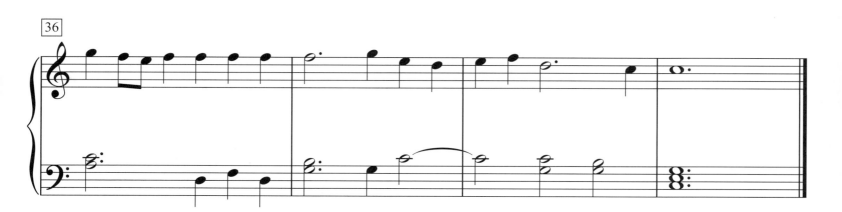

SPRING

FROM THE FOUR SEASONS

By ANTONIO VIVALDI
(1678–1741)

Largo from Symphony No. 9
("New World")

By ANTONIN DVOŘÁK
(1841–1904)

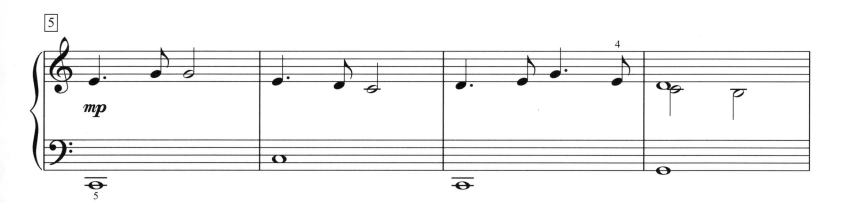

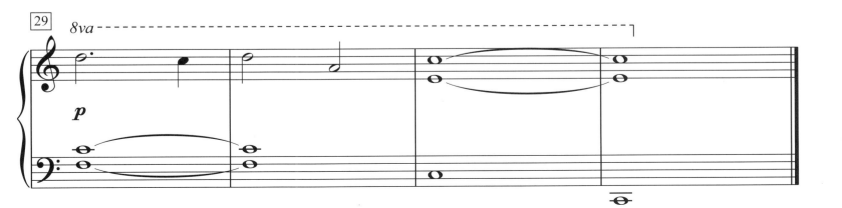

Liebestraum No. 3
(Dream of Love)

By FRANZ LISZT
(1811–1886)

Moderately

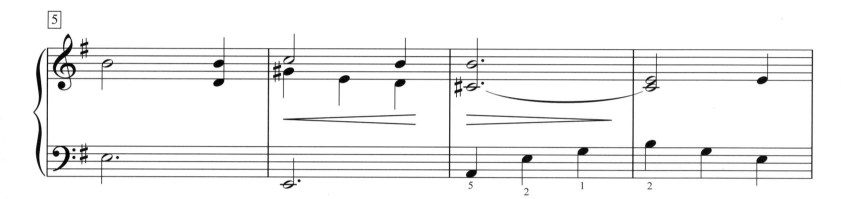

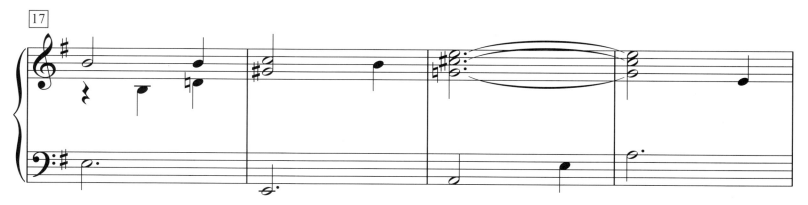

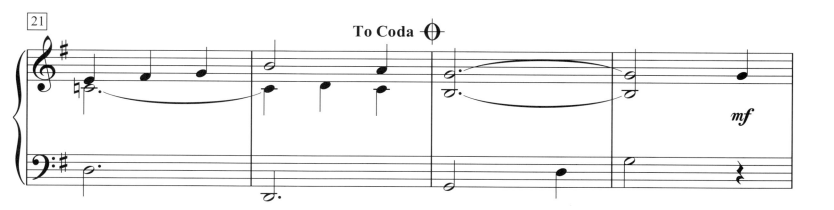

D.S. al Coda

CODA

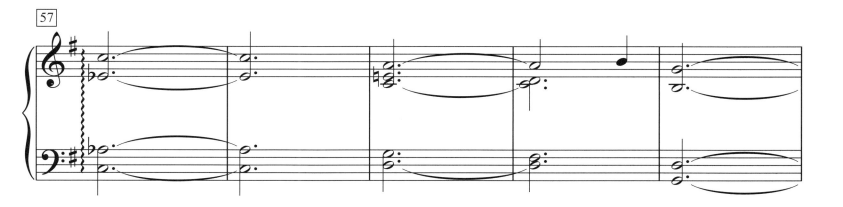

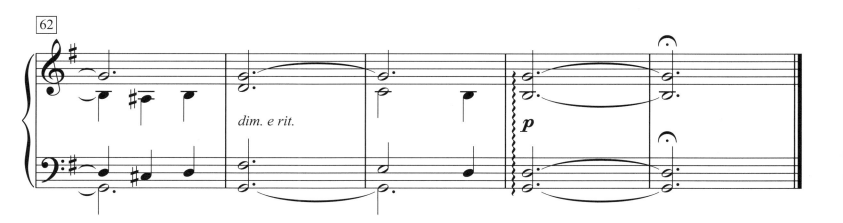

Morning

FROM PEER GYNT

By EDVARD GRIEG
(1843–1907)

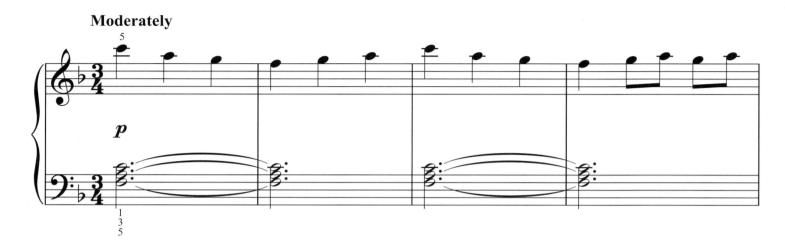

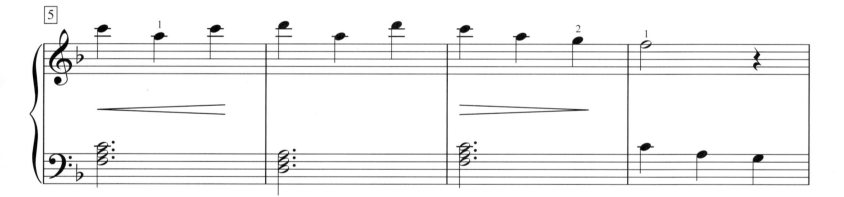

Pavane for the Sleeping Beauty

FROM MOTHER GOOSE SUITE

By MAURICE RAVEL
(1875–1937)

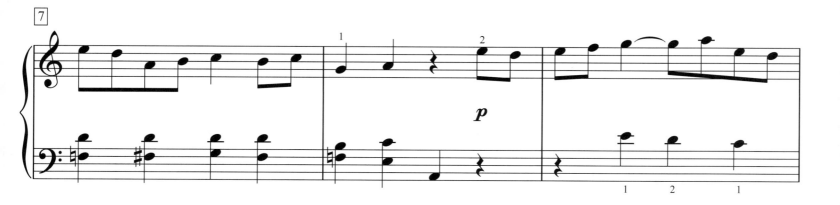

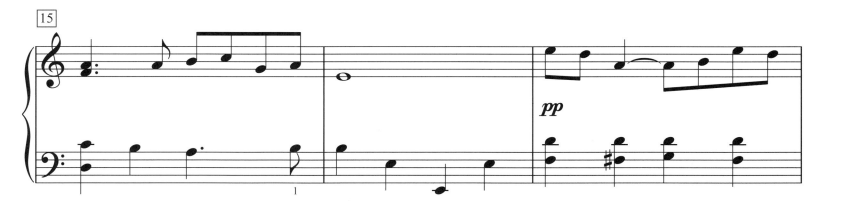

Pomp and Circumstance

By EDWARD ELGAR
(1857–1934)

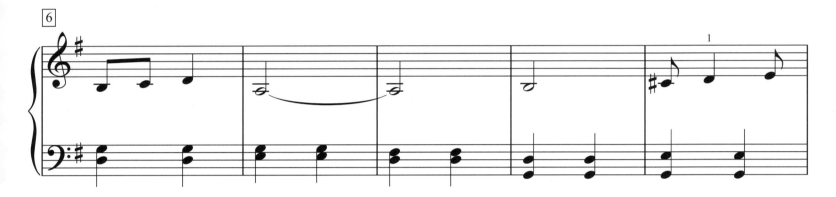

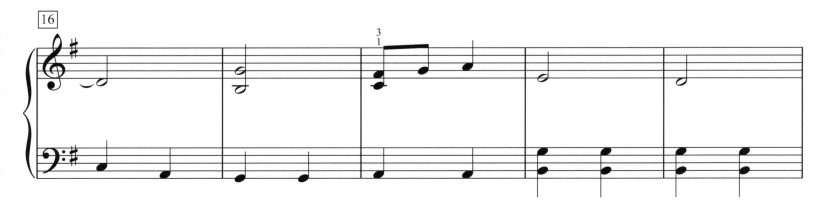

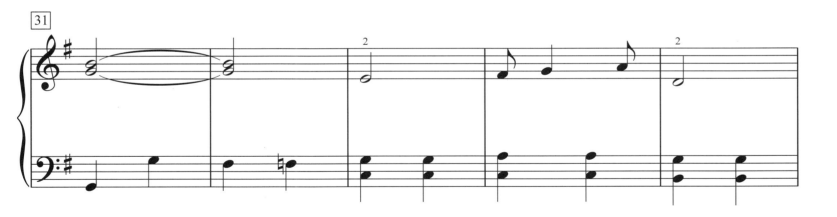

PROMENADE THEME

FROM PICTURES AT AN EXHIBITION

By MODEST MOUSSORGSKY
(1839–1881)

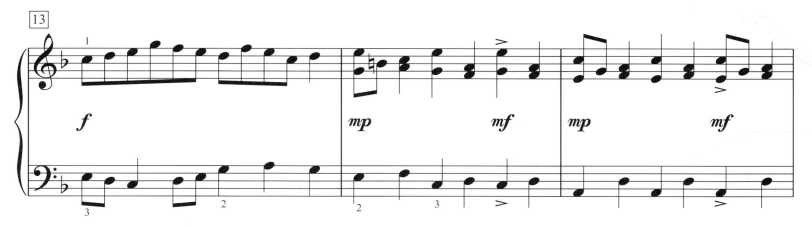

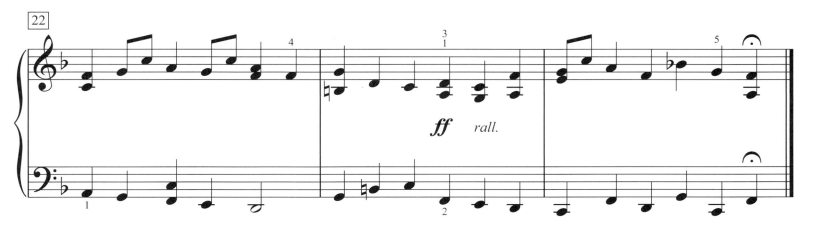

RHAPSODY IN BLUE

By GEORGE GERSHWIN
(1898–1937)

Freely

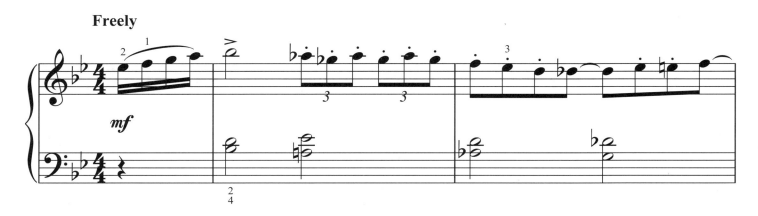

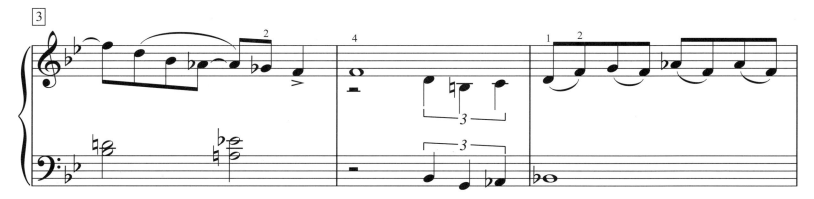

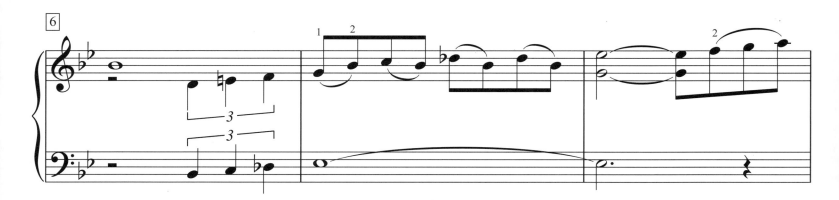

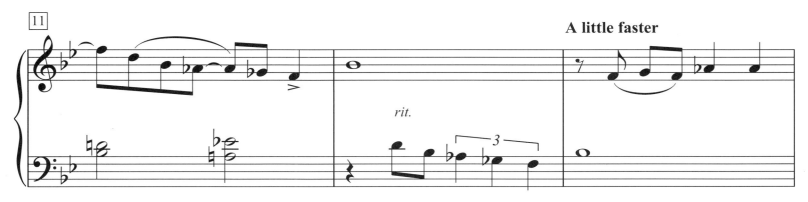

A little faster

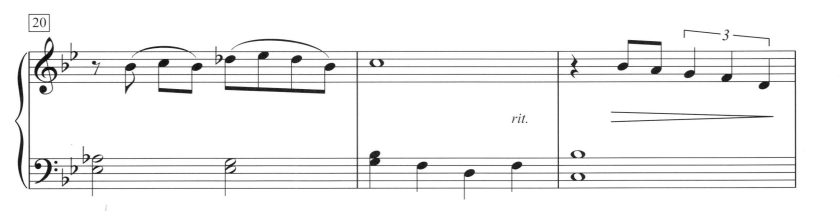

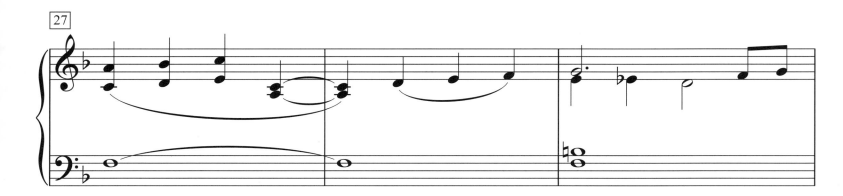

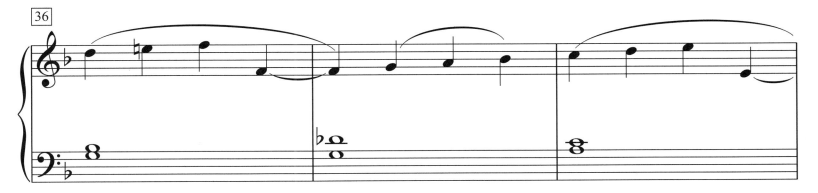

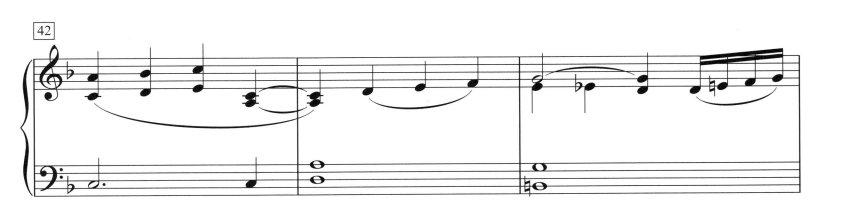

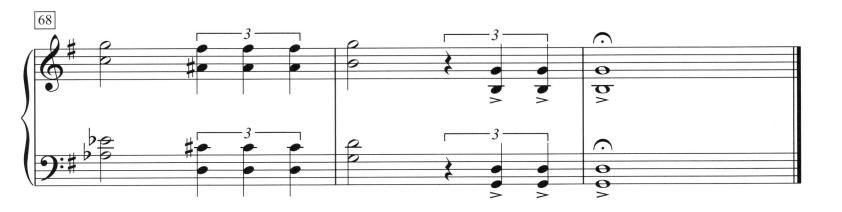

Ride of the Valkyries

FROM DIE WALKÜRE

By RICHARD WAGNER
(1813–1883)

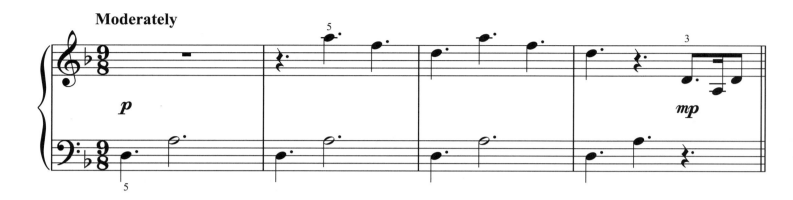

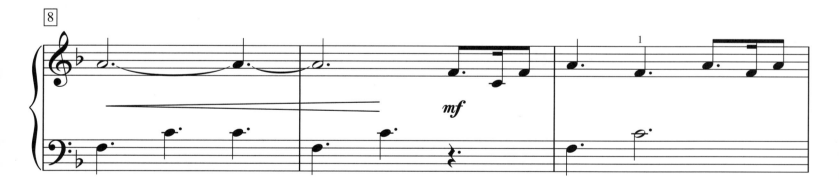

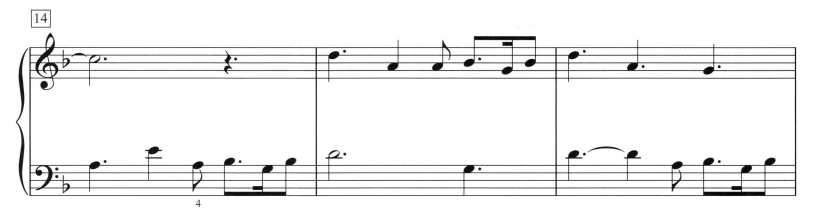

SLEEPING BEAUTY WALTZ

By PYOTR IL'YICH TCHAIKOVSKY
(1840–1893)

Moderate Waltz, in 1

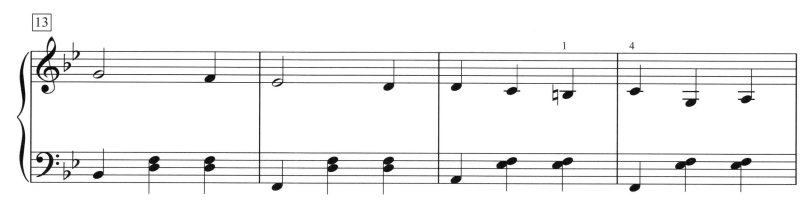

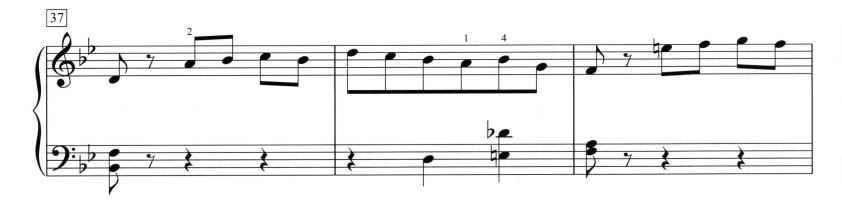

D.C. al Coda

CODA

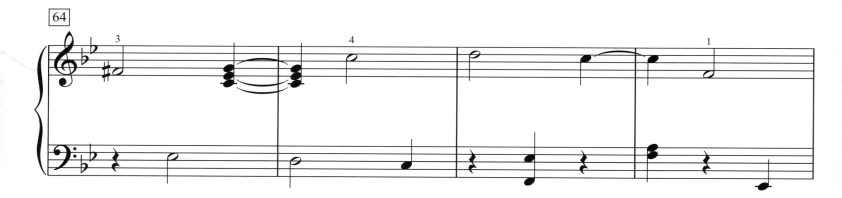

The Swan

FROM CARNIVAL OF THE ANIMALS

By CAMILLE SAINT-SAËNS
(1835–1921)

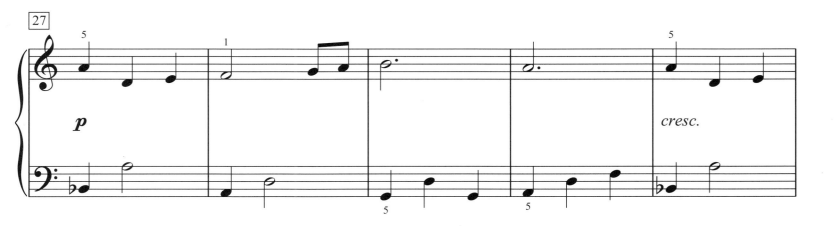

70

STARS AND STRIPES FOREVER

By JOHN PHILIP SOUSA
(1854–1932)

Steady March

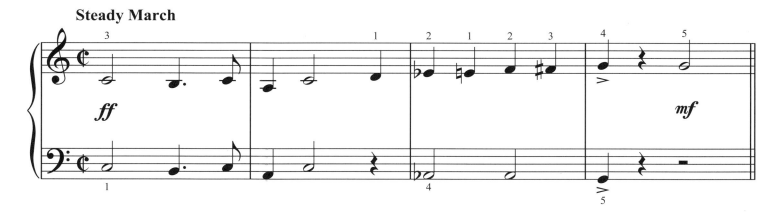

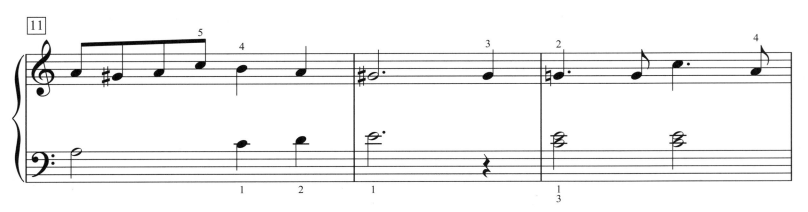

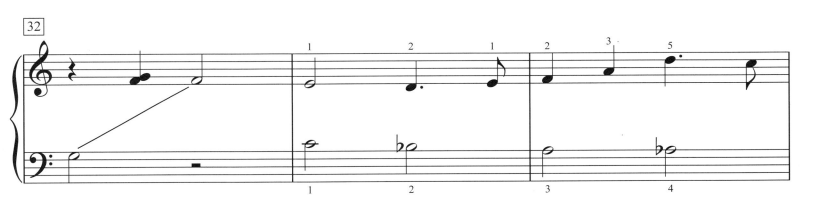

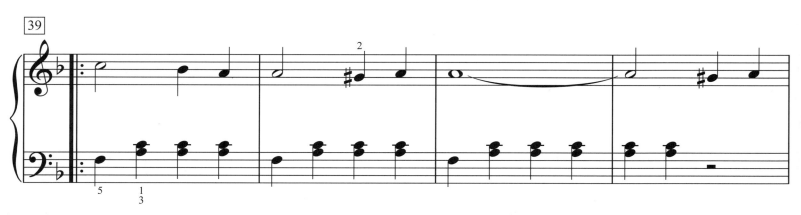

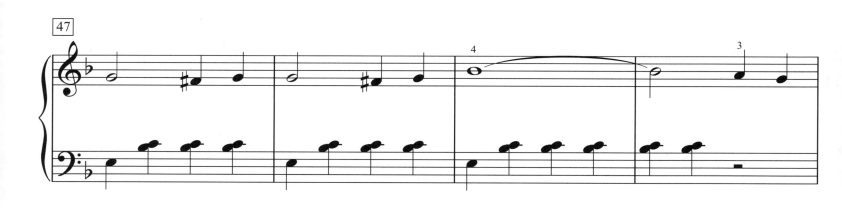

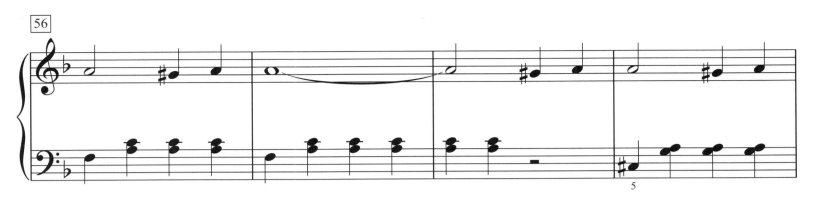

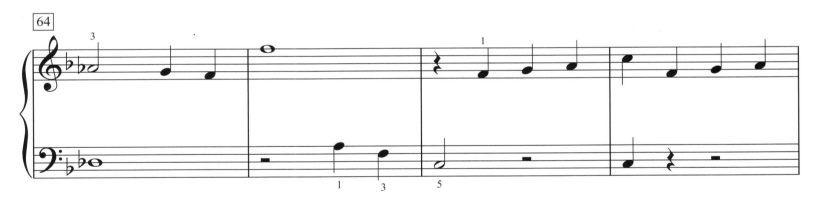

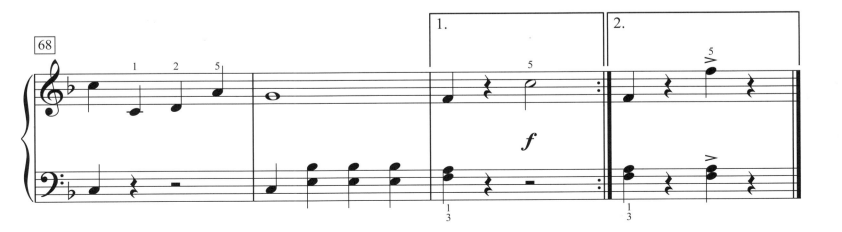

Symphony No. 5

First Movement Themes

By LUDWIG VAN BEETHOVEN
(1770–1827)

Allegro con brio

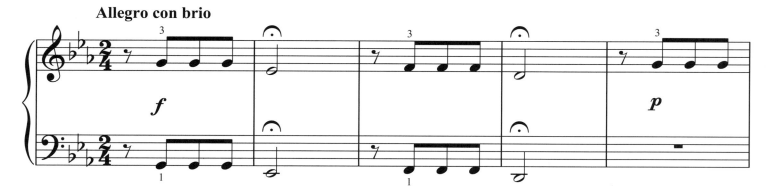

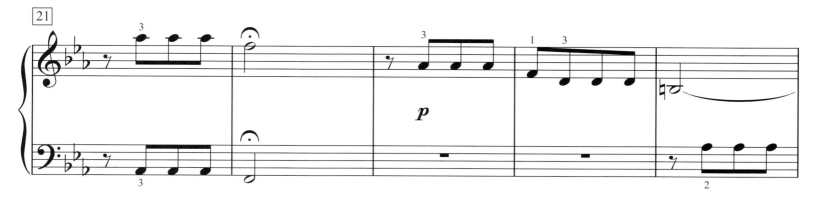

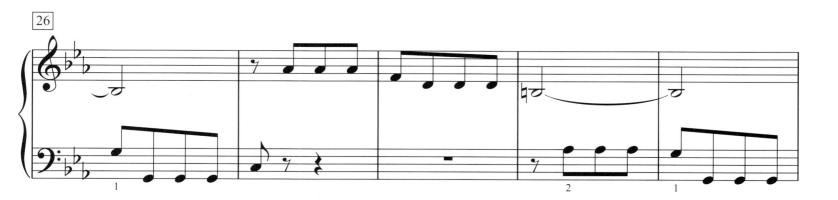

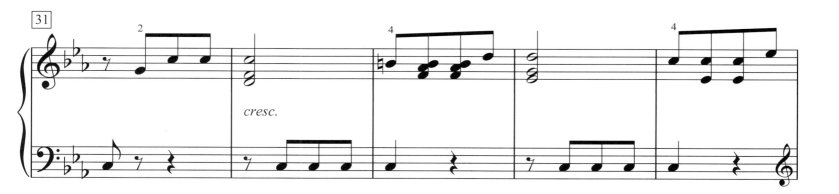

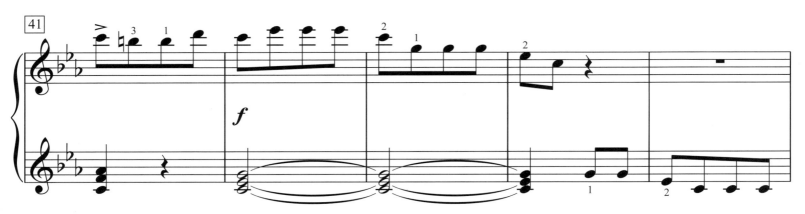

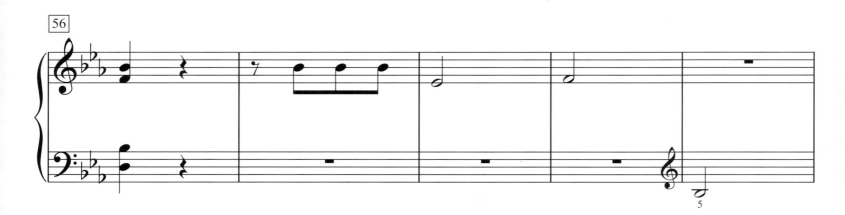

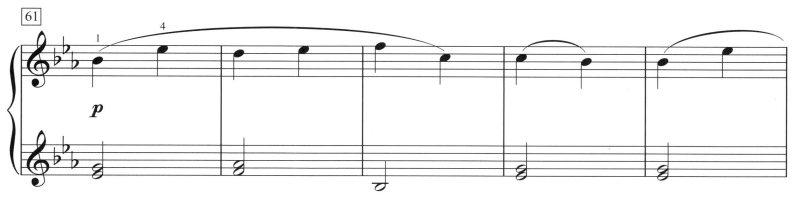

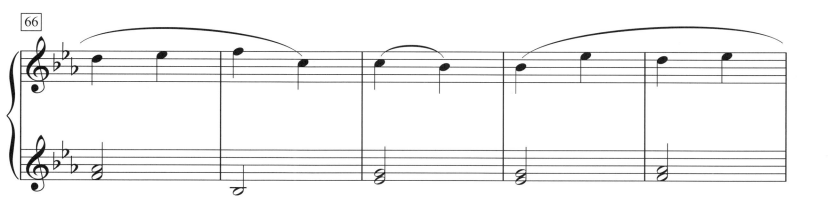

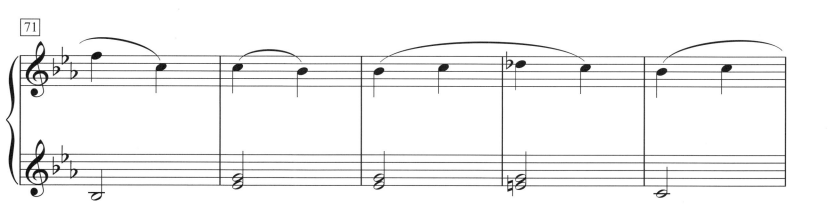

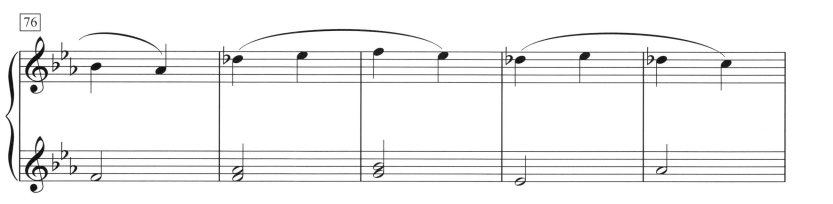

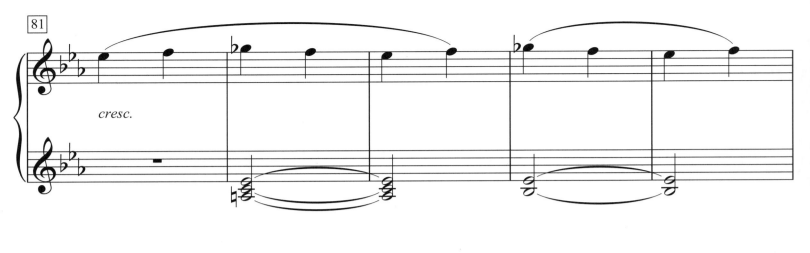

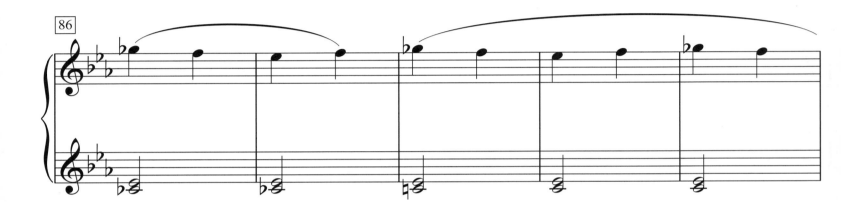

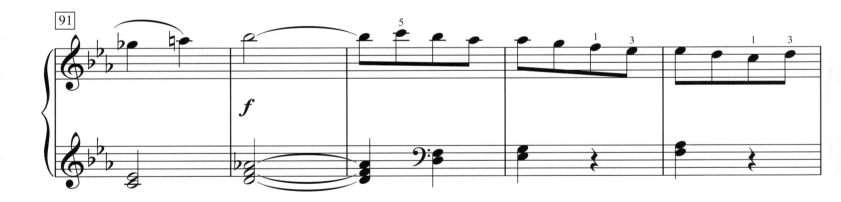

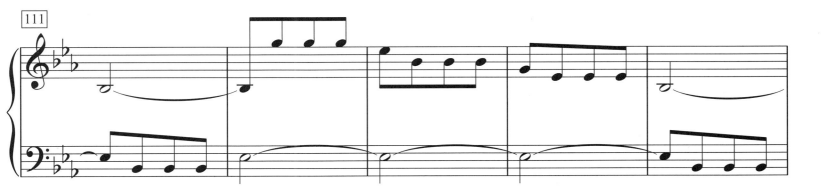

Träumerei
(Dreaming)

FROM SCENES FROM CHILDHOOD

By ROBERT SCHUMANN
(1810–1856)

Slowly, with expression

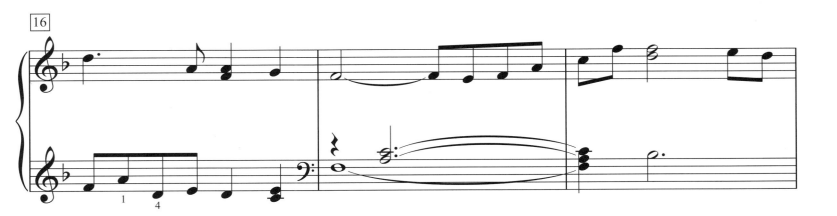

William Tell Overture

By GIOACHINO ROSSINI
(1792–1868)

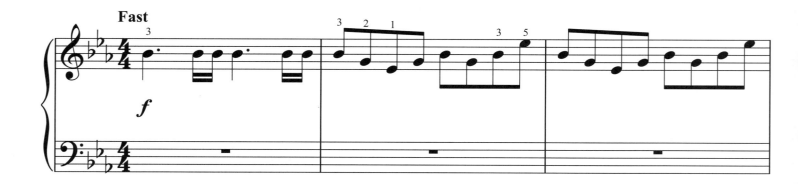

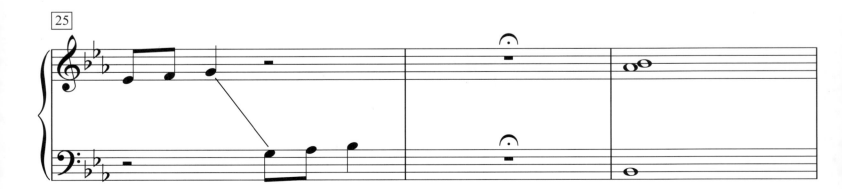

TOREADOR SONG

FROM CARMEN

By GEORGES BIZET
(1838–1875)

Moderately